Listen, Son

Nihil Obstat
Rev. John J. Clifford, S.J.
Censor Dept.
July 29, 1952

†

Imprimatur
† Samuel Cardinal Stritch
Archbishop of Chicago
July 30, 1952

Listen, Son

▼

A Father's Talks on the Facts
of Life and Catholic Ideals
of Social Conduct

▼

IN THREE PARTS

ANGELUS PRESS

2918 TRACY AVENUE
KANSAS CITY, MISSOURI 64109
PHONE (816) 753-3150
FAX   (816) 753-3557

ISBN 0-935952-97-7

Printed in the United States of America.

In deepest humility

this little work is dedicated to

GOD THE HOLY GHOST

with a fervent prayer

that He may enlighten and direct

all who read it.

FOREWORD

WE LIVE in an age of practical paganism. There are still, it is true, many Christians who lead a truly Christian life; even many of our government officials pay external homage to God; and there are numerous evidences that religion still exerts an influence on individuals and on society. Yet the general condition of family life, the godlessness of our public schools, the trends in both private and commercialized amusements, the dominant tone of the vast majority of best sellers, magazines and papers and the character of popular songs all paint an over-all picture of a world that is not much concerned about God or the affairs of another life.

It is into this world that the children of today are born. It is this world in which they grow up, with which they daily rub elbows and which day in and day out, in a thousand different ways, helps to affect their outlook on life, fix their standards, form their habits, shape their objectives and plans, and mold their character. It is like the current of a vast swift stream that sweeps along everything that floats on its surface.

Is there any way to counteract the influence of these forces of ungodliness? Any means of holding fast to Catholic principles and practices despite the seductions of the world? We know that there must be; for God still demands that we keep His commandments, and it is impossible to do so without going counter to the ways of the world.

Probably the most important single means to be employed in stemming the tide of worldliness is for parents to inculcate Christian principles in their sons and daughters and regulate their home and social life strictly by these standards. Many a Catholic father no doubt sincerely desires to form the mind and heart of his sons according to Christian standards and to convince them that it is for their own good not to follow the crowd; but he lacks the ability to guide them safely amid the mass of conflicting views and to defend the Christian principles that he desires to teach. He knows the truths of the Catechism but what he needs is a short guidebook applying its truths to everyday life, especially in the difficult and delicate field of sexual and social conduct. It was for the benefit of such fathers and their sons that this series of instructions was written. In twelve heart-to-heart talks, which the father needs only to read to his son, a simple, clear, reverent and graduated account is given of the facts that a growing boy should gradually learn to know.

It is true that a number of books already exist that were written for the express purpose of informing Catholic boys about the facts of life; but apparently none has yet met with general satisfaction. Since the publication of MOTHER's LITTLE HELPER some years ago for the instruction of girls, numerous requests have reached the publishers for a similar set of booklets for boys. It would seem, then, that the books so far written do not adequately meet the demand for a book of this type. One priest made the following observation on MOTHER's LITTLE HELPER: "All other books of this kind that I have read seemed either too spiritual or not spiritual enough. These instructions keep everything on a high plane and still give clear and satisfactory explanations and reasons."

The present little work, accordingly, is intended to be the aid to Catholic fathers that MOTHER's LITTLE HELPER has been to literally hundreds of thousands of Catholic mothers during the past dozen years. Like its elder companion, it carefully avoids the use of crass anatomical and biological terms; and by constantly referring to the fact that man is the work of God and that every detail of his origin and development has been ordained by God's infinite wisdom, strives to make the child realize that God alone is the author and master of life and, therefore, that all the processes of life are as sacred as they are mysterious and admirable.

Unless a boy acquires the supernatural attitude toward this subject right in the beginning, there will be danger of his having a wrong attitude towards it all through life. But if the subject is introduced and unfolded to him by his own parent in a tactful and reverent manner with constant reference to God and a minimum of physical details, the first impression he receives will be sacred, deep and lasting; and he will be prepared to acquire more detailed information from other Catholic sources whenever his age or circumstances require it.

The generally accepted principles among Catholics in regard to the imparting of sex information can be summarily stated as follows: 1. It should be imparted by the parents; 2. It should be graduated to the child's growing needs; 3. Details should be given to single individuals, not to a group, and above all, not to a mixed group; 4. The information should be accompanied with suggestions of motives and means for the practice of purity. To enable parents to observe the spirit of these rules, there should be separate books for the instructions of boys and for the instructions of girls; and sex information of importance for adolescents of only one sex should be excluded from books intended for the instruction of the opposite sex.

An earnest effort has been made to make LISTEN, SON, conform to all these requirements. Not only is the matter specialized for the boy, but it is graduated both by age groups and by stages in the several age groups. Every effort should be made, however, that the rights of the parents in this regard be respected, and especially that the great advantages of the son's receiving these instructions from his parent be safeguarded. It is for this reason that these booklets are being distributed privately and not advertised in papers or periodicals circulating among the general public.

All who may co-operate in bringing these instructions to the attention of parents are urgently requested to respect the designs of the publishers and not place the booklets in pamphlet racks or otherwise permit them to be sold indiscriminately. It is a strange inconsistency to tell parents to instruct their children, and then to hand the children a pamphlet that gives them at one sitting all the information that their parents are wisely giving them at greater or lesser intervals. But to put a book on sex in a pamphlet rack is to incite the young folks to read it; and if an immature reader suffers harm from it, someone besides the reader will share the responsibility.

The age at which the first instruction may best be read to any particular boy, as well as how long an interval should elapse before the reading of each successive instruction, will naturally depend upon the type of boy and each one's peculiar circumstances. The proverb "Where ignorance is bliss, 'tis folly to be wise," still has its justification, especially since experience proves that too early initiation into the mysteries of life does not make a boy truly wise, but produces rather that undesirable and preposterous thing—the sophisticated child. Even in this age in which the atmosphere seems charged with sex, many perfectly normal, wideawake and lively boys find so many things absorbing their interest that they never pay any attention to sex; and some even pass the middle of their teens without ever thinking to inquire where babies come from.

Still, as a rule, the first instruction had probably best be given when a boy reaches his ninth year, even though he may have asked no questions nor manifested any curiosity about the origin of life. The remaining instructions can then follow the schedule of years given on the title page of each booklet, unless some circumstance should make it advisable to anticipate the suggested schedule. A point to be noted is that all the instructions are to be read by the father to his son and not simply given to him to read for himself. Some fathers may prefer to study the contents and then give the substance in their own words or recite the instruction from memory. But many will not feel capable of adopting that method, as the right word that seemed so inevitable in reading over the instruction often fails to come to mind on repeating the lesson. Then, too, the very fact that the matter is being read from an approved Catholic book will lend it additional authority in the eyes of the boy.

The main reason why the booklet should not be given to the boy to read is that he should be trained to confide in his father in regard to all problems of the years of his adolescence, and an occasional heart-to-heart talk with his boy is one of the best means the father can use of winning and preserving his confidence. For the same reason, if there are two or more sons of nearly the same age in the family, the talks should nevertheless be given to each separately, so that each may have the father's whole attention and an opportunity to ask questions without being embarrassed by the presence of others. Though they should be encouraged to ask questions and mention their doubts, they should also be given to understand that, if it is deemed advisable to postpone the answer, they should be content and not seek information elsewhere, as their father will tell them all that will be useful for them at the proper time.

One last word of caution may not be superfluous; viz., that the instructions should be given at a time when the boy is in a quiet mood and disposed to receive them. He will not be disposed if he is forced to sit down and listen when he is dying to be somewhere else. The father should choose a time when both are at leisure, gain his interest by some paternal remark (which might well be a compliment or a word of appreciation), and then invite him aside for a little chat. The mother can co-operate by arranging to have the other children occupied elsewhere; and both parents should recommend the matter to God in prayer both before and during, as well as after, the conference.

PART ONE

(To be read to boys of from 9 to 13 years)

INSTRUCTION I

Listen, son.

One of the very first things you learned in Religion class was the answer to the question: "Who made you?" You were taught that God made you: that He made heaven and earth, the land and the sea, plants and animals and all things. Later on you were told *how* God made the first man and the first woman. The first man, Adam, God made by making a body out of earth and breathing into it an immortal soul. And Eve, the first woman, God made out of a rib which He took from Adam's side while he was asleep.

You were never told how God made all other men and women; but you know that they must be made in a different way than Adam and Eve, because God made Adam at once a full-grown man and Eve a full-grown woman; while all other men and women come into the world as babies.

Now have you never wondered how God makes babies, and where they come from? Perhaps you did ask your mother sometime where babies come from; and she probably told you that they come from God, which is perfectly true. But things come from God in different ways.

You see, son, when we say that God made all things, or that He is the Creator of all things, we do not mean that He made everything directly out of nothing. God made the peaches and the apples, which you like to eat, and the roses, which you love to see; but you know that they are not made directly out of nothing, because you have seen them growing on trees and bushes. At first the peach tree produced buds; the buds grew into blossoms, and the blossoms into peaches. And even the tree itself was not made out of nothing; because you know very well that trees, like plants and flowers, grow up out of seeds. Yet it is entirely correct to say that God made them, because in the beginning, thousands of years ago, God created the first trees and plants and flowers, and made them so that each one would produce seed from which other trees and plants would develop.

Thus God is the Creator of all things, since He made everything either directly out of nothing or indirectly by making certain things produce other things of the same kind. This shows the greatness of God's power. Men can make flowers, too, that is, artificial ones: and they can make them so perfect that you can hardly distinguish them from natural ones. But no man can make a flower that will grow and have seeds and produce other flowers.

This is all very interesting to you, I am sure; but the most interesting thing is how God makes man. Every day thousands of new children come into the world. Do they just drop into their cradles out of the air like the lovely snowflakes that fall from the sky? Or do their Guardian Angels bring them down from Heaven and place them in the arms of their mothers? No. God could create them in that way if He wanted to, but He doesn't. There are many ways in which God could bring children into the world, but He chose only one way; and since He is infinitely wise and holy, the way He chose must surely be the best. But what is that way?

When God creates a new human being, instead of making its body, as He did Adam's out of earth, He makes it out of a substance which He prepares in the body of its mother. In the very same instant that the tiny body is formed, God makes an immortal soul directly out of nothing and unites it to the body. This tiny living body is then nourished and developed inside its mother's body until the time comes for it to be born.

It was in this way that the Son of God Himself became man, as you can see from the Gospel that is read on the feast of the Annunciation of the Blessed Virgin. "The Angel Gabriel," so we read there, "was sent by God into a city of Galilee called Nazareth to a virgin espoused to a man whose name was Joseph, of the house of David. And the virgin's name was Mary. And the Angel being come in, said to her: "Hail, full of grace, the Lord is with thee. Blessed art thou among women. . . . Behold, thou shalt conceive in thy womb and shalt bring forth a son, and He shall be called the "Son of the Most High.' . . . And Mary said: 'Behold the handmaid of the Lord; be it done to me according to thy word" (Luke 1, 26-38).

As soon as Mary uttered these words, she conceived by the Holy Ghost, as we say in the Angelus; that means, by the action of the Holy Ghost the body and soul of Jesus were made in Mary's womb and united to the Second Person of the Blessed Trinity. So you see that the sublime mystery of the Incarnation of the Son of God was accomplished in the chaste womb of the immaculate Virgin Mary. The womb, you must know, is that organ inside a woman's body in which a child is conceived, that is, brought into existence, then nourished just as its mother is nourished by the food that she eats, and from which it is finally brought forth or born and then nourished at its mother's breast. And as Jesus was formed in the womb of His Blessed Mother, so every child that comes into the world is also formed inside the body of its mother.

So now you know how God creates little children; and you now understand, too, why a mother loves her child so much, since the child's body was formed out of her own substance and fed with milk at her breast. But now listen, son. I never spoke to you about this before, because the creation of a child is something so wonderful that boys and girls are usually not told about it until they are old enough to appreciate the information. Then, too, it is a very mysterious and sacred subject, which young folks do not know how to talk about in the right way. But you are now supposed to be old enough and to have sense enough to keep this information to yourself and not to speak about it to anyone but your parents or your confessor. From time to time, I intend to give you other instructions on this subject and on other subjects; and I want you to feel free to ask me any questions that may come to your mind. You can be sure that your mother and I want to do all that we can for you, not only to make you happy and help you grow up healthy and strong, but also to help you grow up a good boy. So trust us and don't try to get information from other persons, because we will tell you all that it will be good for you to know at the proper time.

INSTRUCTION II

My dear son.

In the instruction I gave you some time ago, I explained to you that Our Lord was conceived in His Blessed Mother's womb on the day of the Annunciation. From that day until He was born, Jesus lay hidden away beneath his Mother's heart. If you recall how happy you were the first time you received Jesus in Holy Communion, you can imagine how much greater must have been the joy that Mary felt. For the consecrated Host that you receive remains in you only a short time; but Jesus remained in Mary for nine months; so that during all that time Mary knew that, no matter where she went or what she did, whether working or praying, walking or sleeping, she had Little Jesus within her.

As the Annunciation is celebrated on March 25, you will now understand why Christmas or the birth of our Lord is celebrated on December 25—just nine months later. Nine months usually pass by from the time that a child is conceived until it is born; and during that time the mother is said to be "with child" or to be an "expectant" mother. As the Blessed Virgin knew from the annunciation of the Angel Gabriel the exact day that Jesus was conceived, she knew also when He was to be born; and she accordingly took with her the necessary infant clothing when she had to journey to Bethlehem. Other women are not so fortunate as to know at once when God has given them a child; but after a few weeks it is indicated by certain physical signs, and they can then figure out approximately when the child may be expected to be born.

It is to these facts of nature that the evangelist St. Luke refers when he says in the Gospel of the first Mass on Christmas Day: "And Joseph also went up from Galilee . . . to Bethlehem to be enrolled with Mary, his espoused wife.

who was with child. And it came to pass that when they were there, her days were accomplished that she should be delivered. And she brought forth her first-born Son, and wrapped Him up in swaddling clothes and laid Him in a manger" (Luke 2, 6-7).

As Mary carried Jesus under her heart for nine months, so Mary had been carried in like manner by her mother St. Ann for the same length of time. You will find, therefore, if you count the months, that there were exactly nine months also between the Immaculate Conception of the Blessed Virgin and her Nativity, since the former is celebrated on December 8, and the latter on September 8. It may be well to remind you here what is meant by the Immaculate Conception. When other children are conceived, their souls are stained with original sin; but because God created Mary's soul in the state of sanctifying grace, we say that she was conceived without sin, or that her conception was immaculate. It is to honor this great privilege of Mary's Immaculate Conception that the Church has attached an indulgence of 300 days to the little prayer: "O Mary, conceived without sin, pray for us who have recourse to thee." Learn this prayer by heart and say it often, especially when you are tempted to do anything wrong. Mary is your heavenly Mother, and she loves you even more than your mother and I do.

Since you learned about the way that God creates children, the thought may have come to you: I wonder how it comes that only married women have children. There are several things that must be explained to you in answer to that question; but the most important thing is this: Bringing up children, taking proper care of them, obtaining food, clothing and shelter for them, and training and instructing them is by no means an easy task. For this reason, and no doubt for other wise reasons, God in His infinite wisdom and fatherly care for His Children, arranged that every child should have also a father, who should love it, labor to support it and its mother, provide a home for them, and form with them a family. And that the parents might not separate and deprive the child of the loving care that it needs. God also ordained that the parents should be united in marriage and be bound by the marriage contract to live together until death.

Another thing that you may have wondered about is why a doctor is usually called when a baby is born. You may even have heard people say: "The doctor brought us a new baby." This does not mean that the doctor brought the baby into the home, but that he helped the mother bring it into the world. You see, son, a mother usually suffers great pain and sometimes has great difficulty in giving birth to a child; and a new-born baby is a very delicate creature. For these reasons it is advisable and at times even necessary to have a doctor to assist the mother and to give her and her infant the best of care. That is why it is very common nowadays for women to go to a hospital when they expect the birth of a child. If Adam and Eve had not sinned, giving birth to a child would have been easy and painless; but in punishment for their sin, God addressed to Eve the following words: "In sorrow shalt thou bring forth children." And that is also what Our Lord referred to when He said to His Apostles: "A woman when she is about to give birth, hath sorrow because her hour is come; but when she hath brought forth the child, she remembereth no more the anguish for joy that a man is born into the world" (John 16, 21).

INSTRUCTION III

Listen, son.

After I told you that God creates children within their mother's body, I said that God wanted only married women to have babies so that the children would have both a father and a mother to love them and to take care of them. It does not follow from that, however, that all married women have children. Some women are married for years without having any, although they would dearly love to have children. Thus St. Ann, the wife of St. Joachim, had no child until she was quite old, when she became the mother of the Blessed Virgin. Just why this is so, no one fully understands; but usually there is some physical cause, just as there is some physical cause why some people remain small and others grow tall; some get stout and some stay thin.

In some cases, however, married women have no children because they do not do what is necessary to have a child. You see, since it is a lot of trouble for parents to take care of their children, God does not give them a child unless they do what is necessary to have one. So if they do not do that, they will never have any children.

Another reason why God wants the parents to cooperate with Him in the creation of new human beings is that He wants the parents to have a great love for their children; and everybody naturally loves what he himself helped to make. Thus a boy is much attached to a radio, a toy or perhaps a drawing or painting he has made himself. And if he worked long and hard at a picture or something in order to make a gift of it to his parents, we say that it was a work of love.

Now God in His infinite wisdom wanted every child to be also a work of love—the result of the love of husband and wife for each other. For this reason He has made it natural for certain men and women to love each other more than any other person, or as we say, to fall in love with each other, and then to get married by promising to live together and to love each other until death. Since the child is formed of the mother's own substance, as I have already told you, in a little nest, as it were, which God prepares beneath every woman's heart, it is only natural that a mother loves her child as her own self. But God wants the father also to have a share in bringing the child into existence. The father can just as truly say: "This is my child" as the mother; for without the father the child could not have come into being. The only child who never had a real human father was the Child Jesus. God worked a special miracle to create His body in the womb of the Blessed Virgin; and that is why St. Joseph is called only the foster father of Jesus.

But what does the father's part in bringing the child into existence consist in? It consists in an act of love. You know, I am sure, that a kiss is an act of love. And because God wants husband and wife to love each other more than any other person, it is natural and proper for them to show their love to each other by kissing. But the most intimate act of love is embracing; and it is by a very intimate embrace of his wife that a husband makes it possible for her to become a mother.

You see then, son, how wonderfully and beautifully God has arranged everything for the creation of a child. He wants every child to be the result of the love that its father and mother have for each other.

Yet, holy and sacred as is this embrace in the married state, it is not lawful for unmarried persons. Even kisses between young men and young women are often sinful because they may lead to this embrace; but the intimate embrace itself that is permitted to a husband and his wife would always be a mortal sin for unmarried persons. You can easily understand what a difference marriage makes, if you recall what a difference the Sacrament of Holy Orders makes. A priest is a human being just as well as a layman is; yet because the priest has received Holy Orders, it is a holy and sacred thing for him to touch and handle the Sacred Host, while for an unordained person the same act would be a mortal sin and a sacrilege.

Still, since it is possible for an unmarried girl to allow a man to give her the marital embrace, it is possible also for an unmarried girl to become a mother. But, as I have said, in that case such an embrace would be a grievous sin for the boy as well as for the girl. It would not be a sin, of course, for the girl, if a man would overpower her and give her that embrace entirely against her will. But such a thing does not happen so easily, as the girl would know at once that he was doing something wrong and she could offer resistance. Still, because of the danger, a boy should beware of being all alone with a girl in a place where they can not be seen by others; e.g., in a car parked in a dark place.

Here let me warn you again not to talk about these things with other boys; and if they begin to do so, talk of something else or go away. As I told you in the first instruction, this is a sacred subject, and boys are too lightminded to speak of it with proper reverence. Besides, you still do not know enough about it, and if you speak of it with them, you may give them wrong ideas or get wrong ideas from them. All through life we have to control our curiosity in regard to some things; so learn to control your curiosity about this matter for the love of God. Remember what happened to Eve for being over curious and accepting information from the wrong source. Instead of believing what God told her, she believed the serpent and ate of the forbidden fruit. A bad boy can also be like a snake in the grass; so whenever you want any information on this subject, don't go to boys, but ask your parents, and they will tell you all that will be useful for you in good time.

INSTRUCTION IV

My dear son.

It is customary in many Catholic schools, for the Sisters to collect pennies from the pupils for the purchase of Chinese babies. The pupils are told that in far off China many pagan mothers care so little for their children that when they have more children than they want, they will put a new-born babe out on the street to die; but if they are paid a small sum of money, they will let the Catholic missionaries take the child and baptize it and bring it up a Christian. The abandoning of their children by these Chinese mothers no doubt seems very strange to you, but as they are pagans and live so far away, you probably think that the destruction of infant lives is something that occurs only among uncivilized nations.

I wish it were possible to leave you under that impression always. But you will not be a child always. You will grow up and will have to act your part on the stage of life. And as life is a serious business, you must be instructed how to act. You might be told what you have to expect, so that you will not be taken by surprise and in your confusion make serious mistakes.

Since, therefore, you are developing rapidly and will soon be passing from boyhood to youth or young manhood, it is now time for you to be told that terrible wickedness is found not only in far distant pagan countries or in nations of long ago, but right here in our own country; yes, even in your own city, and perhaps even among people who are looked upon as upright and respectable citizens. You might gasp at the idea and think it impossible; yet it is only too true that hundreds of babies are killed in this country every year.

This shows how wicked people can become when they do not listen to the teachings of religion. If a human life gets in the way of their desire for ease, comfort or pleasure, and they can do away with it without being punished by civil authorities, they simply do away with it. In this instruction, then, I want to speak to you about the sacredness of human life, so that you will understand better what an awful crime it is detroy even a single human life. It is true, the willful killing of a grown-up person or even of a child in cold blood is regarded with horror by all civilized people. But many people do not consider it a serious thing to destroy the life of an unborn child; and it was chiefly of unborn children that I was speaking when I said that many children are killed in this country every year.

Probably the main reason why many people do not think it a serious matter to destroy the life of an unborn child, is the fact that the child is not fully developed and has never been seen, and in consequence is not missed. Then, too, since in the early months of its life before birth, a child can often be got rid of very easily merely by means of certain drugs or medicines, a woman who does not want to bother with a baby thinks it a very simple thing to take a little medicine and get rid of it, that is, murder it. I say murder, for no matter how innocent the taking of medicine may seem to be, to take it for the purpose of destroying the life of an unborn child is nothing less than willful murder; just as much as it would be to give deadly poison to a child already born.

You see, son, from the very first moment that God creates a soul and unites it to a body in the mother's womb, that tiny creature (smaller at first that a sparkling dewdrop) is a real human being—a being endowed with understanding and free will, a being that will exist for all eternity. And since it is a human being, it has a strict right to its life, just as truly as the aged man or hopeless invalid who is no longer able to take care of himself; and, therefore, it has also a strict right to the nourishment and care it needs in order to live and grow and be born. And not only the child has a right to its life which no one can dispute, but, more so still, God has a right to its life which no one can violate without committing a grievous sin.

When God created man, He gave him power over the lives of irrational animals; but the power over the lives of men God reserved to Himself. Consequently, when amid thunder and lightning on Mount Sinai God solemnly declared, "Thou shalt not kill," He forbade the killing of every human being, whether old or young, sick or well, born or unborn, except in a few cases where it is permitted in self-defense, in a just war, or by lawful authority for the punishment of a serious crime.

You can understand now that, if it is a great wrong for a pagan mother to expose her newborn babe to the danger of death, it must be a far greater crime for a Catholic woman to kill her unborn child. For the pagan mother knows nothing of the necessity of being baptized in order to get to Heaven; but a Catholic mother knows that by killing the child in her womb she not only robs it of life, but robs it also of all chance of ever going to Heaven. God created the soul of that child for the eternal happiness of Heaven; Jesus died on the cross that He might wash original sin from its soul with His Precious Blood; and the Holy Ghost wished to clothe it with the beautiful robe of sanctifying grace. If in spite of knowing all this, a Catholic mother deliberately prevents her child from obtaining all those blessings, she just as much as says: "I don't care if God did create this child for Heaven, or if Jesus did die for it, or if the Holy Ghost does want to sanctify it. I don't want to be bothered with it, and so I'll get rid of it." Isn't it awful? Perhaps you still doubt that a Catholic mother can really be so heartless; but it is a sad fact that some of them are at times.

It is true, some women, especially non-Catholic ones, who are guilty of this sin, are not entirely to blame, because they have never been properly instructed on this matter; and, therefore, though their own conscience should, and does, tell them that it is wrong, it does not appear to them to be as wrong as it really is. And very often, too, they are told by other women that it is the proper thing to do if they are poor or if they already have several children to take care of.

The sin of wilfully causing the death of an unborn child is called abortion. If an unborn child is killed by being accidentally forced out of the womb before the proper time, that is called a miscarriage and is no sin, unless the mother was in some way responsible. Another expression that you may come across some time is "birth control" or "birth prevention," which is another grievously sinful way of keeping from having children. The fact that you sometimes find these expressions in Catholic papers is another reason why it seemed advisable to give you this information at the present time. You know now why Catholic editors condemn it and why Catholic priests preach against it.

But what if a mother were extremely poor or sickly and already had a large family? Would it still be wrong for her to practice abortion or birth control? Yes, my son, even then it would be a grievous sin; and not only for the wife, but also for the husband, if he would co-operate with her in preventing the birth or the conception of a child. You must remember that no parents can have a child unless God gives it to them; and if God wants them to have a child, it is His will that they accept it and bring it up for Heaven. Very often it is the last child that is the source of the greatest joy and consolation to its parents. St. Therese of the Child Jesus was her parents' ninth and last child; St. Ignatius of Loyola, the thirteenth.

Although you are only a boy, I am sure that this instruction has made a deep impression upon you. You now realize that there are evils in the world of which you had never dreamed, and that birth prevention is a serious sin, no matter how many people practice it and no matter what they say to defend it. Be careful, however, never to suspect any married couples of being guilty of this sin, if they have only one or two or no children. There are so many innocent reasons why married people may remain childless, that we have no right to judge them guilty of that sin, unless they themselves admit it.

INSTRUCTION V

Listen, son.

Though you may not have given much attention to the fact, you have undoubtedly heard or read at some time that is was an extraordinary privilege for the Blessed Virgin to be at the same time a virgin and a mother. She is, in fact, the only woman that ever became a mother without ceasing to be a virgin. If you have thought about the matter at all, you probably thought that a virgin is the same as an unmarried woman, and that as soon as a virgin marries she is no longer a virgin. That is not the case. A virgin does not cease to be a virgin by the mere fact that she contracts a valid marriage, but by the fact that she and her husband make use of the marriage right, that is, the right to the marital embrace conferred by the Sacrament of Matrimony. And as most married couples make use of that right soon after being married, married women are no longer classed as virgins but as matrons.

From what I told you in a former instruction, you know that no woman can conceive a child naturally or become what is called an expectant mother without the co-operation of the child's father. Hence when Mary had given birth to Jesus, her relatives and friends took it for granted that she had become a mother through the co-operation of St. Joseph in the same natural way as every other mother. Even the Blessed Virgin herself had no idea how she could become a mother in any other way when the angel appeared to her and declared that she would conceive in her womb and bring forth a son. That is why she said to the angel: "How shall this be done, because I do not know man" (Luke 1, 34). By the words "I do not know man," Mary meant that she did not make use of her right to the marital embrace, because she had made the vow of perpetual virginity. The angel then explained to her that she would become the mother of Jesus in a supernatural manner by a special act of the Holy Ghost.

And just as Mary did not understand at first how she could remain a virgin if she became a mother, so neither did St. Joseph. When it became plain to St. Joseph, therefore, from Mary's changed appearance, that she was with child, and he knew full well that he was not the child's father, he decided to leave her, although the very thought of parting from so dear and holy a spouse almost broke his noble heart.

These extraordinary events and how God cleared up the doubts of St. Joseph are narrated by St. Matthew in the Gospel of the feast of St. Joseph in the following manner: "Now the generation of Christ was in this wise. When as His mother Mary was espoused to Joseph, before they came together, she was found with child of the Holy Ghost. Whereupon Joseph, her husband, being a just man and not willing publicly to expose her, was minded to put her away privately. But while he thought on these things, behold the angel of the Lord appeared to him in his sleep, saying, 'Joseph, son of David, fear not to take unto thee Mary, thy wife; for that which is conceived in her is of the Holy Ghost. And she shall bring forth a son, and thou shalt call His name Jesus; for He shall save His people from their sins'" (Matt. 1, 18-21).

It is clear from this Gospel narrative that for a virgin to conceive and become a mother is something so extraordinary that an angel of God had to come to St. Joseph to make him believe it. He knew that if a wife permits another man who is not her husband to embrace her just as if he were her husband, she commits the sin that is called adultery. And as he was sure that Mary was too holy to have committed the slightest sin, he was at a loss how to explain her motherhood, until the angel brought him the happy tidings that she had become the Mother of the Redeemer through the power of the Holy Ghost.

Having mentioned the sin adultery, it will be useful to add here a little further explanation. You know from your catechism that adultery is a sin against the sixth commandment, or a sin of impurity; and it may seem odd to you that what is entirely lawful when done by a husband with his wife, is a sin of impurity if done by the same husband with a woman who is not his wife. I have already told you why such a thing is sinful if done by unmarried persons; namely, because the Sacrament of Matrimony gives certain rights that the unmarried do not have. But even married people have these rights only in regard to their partners in marriage and not in regard to other married persons. They even give a solemn pledge to each other when they marry, not to share those rights with any other person; hence the husband or wife who violates that pledge is said to be unfaithful. It is easy to understand the wisdom of these natural laws; for since it is the duty of the father to provide for his own child, if his wife would consent to the marital embrace of some other man, she would not know which man was the father of her child.

And now, son, I must warn you against making a dangerous mistake. You might suppose, because adultery is the sin of a married person, that the sixth commandment is only for the married, and that unmarried persons cannot sin against the sixth commandment. That would be a grave mistake. You must know that there are two kinds of chastity; virginal chastity or the chastity of the unmarried; and conjugal chastity or the chastity of the married; and a sin against either kind of chastity is called a sin of impurity. Certain kisses and embraces that are permitted to husband and wife would be sins of impurity if done by others. Yet there are certain other actions that are *never* permitted to *anybody* and are always sins of impurity, whether done by a married person or by a single person, whether alone or with another. And the sixth commandment forbids not only adultery, but every kind of impurity.

How I wish you would never need to know anything about this vice! But if you are to be kept from falling into the treacherous quicksand of impurity, you must be told where it is, or at least where you may remain and be sure that you are safe. For this reason, in the following instructions, I shall give you the explanations and warnings that will be useful to you both at the present time and in the future for the preservation of the necessary and beautiful virtue of holy purity. But as you cannot begin the work of defense too soon, let me here give you a few general directions what to do and what to avoid in order to preserve and foster this virtue.

1. *Avoid the occasions of sin.* The Holy Ghost says that he that loveth danger will perish in it. In particular, avoid bad companions (such, for example, as use dirty language), sensational magazines, books and papers; indecent and suggestive pictures, games, dances and other amusements, and all but Class A, No. 1 movies.

2. *Develop your will power,* which you will need to resist temptation, by avoiding idleness and softness. Keep yourself usefully occupied either with work or wholesome recreation, especially outdoors; accustom yourself to hard work, to disagreeable tasks, and to the inclemency of the weather.

3. *Do not be choicy about your food.* Acquire the habit of eating of any kind of wholesome food, but be moderate always, especially in the use of sweets and spices. As to intoxicants, use them rarely and sparingly; or better still, abstain from them altogether, at least until you are 21 years old.

4. *Use the supernatural means of grace,* without which no virtue can long endure. Say your morning and evening prayers regularly and devoutly; cultivate a special devotion to the Blessed Virgin and say three Hail Marys for purity every morning and evening. Go to Holy Communion every Sunday and at least once a week on a weekday; to Confession every two weeks; and seek your confessor's instruction and advice in all doubts and temptations.

PART TWO

(To be read to boys of from 14 to 16 years)

INSTRUCTION VI

Listen, son.

Now that you have reached the age that usually marks the beginning of the change from boyhood to mankind, I think it is about time for me to give you a little talk about this business of growing up. It is a real business, you must know, as you do not change from a boy into a man all at once, just over night as it were. This growing-up process is spread out over a number of years so as to give a boy time to adjust himself properly to his new responsibilities and privileges and to learn to look at life with the eyes of a serious-minded man and not those of a thoughtless boy.

What I am most concerned about is that you do not grow up faster outwardly than you do inwardly: that is, that your body does not develop more rapidly than your soul—than your mind and your will. As the boy Jesus grew in wisdom and age and grace with God and man, so you also should grow and daily become stronger, not merely by increasing the size and strength of your muscles, but also by increasing your store of knowledge and, above all, the strength of your will. A boy has a strong will or great will power when he can easily do things he does not like to do; for example, study his lessons and do his home work when he would like to be outdoors playing; or go to bed and get up promptly at the time his mother wants him to. Boys like to show how strong they are; how much they can lift, how far they can swim or bat a ball; but what really makes a boy manly is that strength of will that enables him to obey his parents readily, control his temper, and at all times be complete master of himself. When a boy has such a will, a will that chooses to do what is right even when it is hard, and refuses to do what is wrong even though most other boys do it, we say that he is a boy of character. He is not a reed shaken by every wind; that is, he is not swayed by his feelings or whims or by what other boys say or think, but only by a sense of duty.

Now is the time for you to begin in earnest to make use of the knowledge you acquired long ago in school. You learned that man is made up of body and soul. That means that there are in us two opposing forces, one material, one spiritual. As St. Paul says, "The flesh lusteth against the spirit, and the spirit against the flesh" (Gal. 5, 17). The soul, being a spirit, values and strives for what is spiritual. Only the soul, for example, can know that God created us for Heaven; and hence only the soul tries to get to Heaven by keeping God's commandments. The body being an animal, with the instincts and cravings of an animal, naturally craves the things that are pleasant to the bodily senses. If you blindly give in to these cravings, e.g., to the appetite for food or the craving for drink, you will eat and drink more than is good for either body or soul. That is why it is necessary that all our bodily cravings be kept under the control of the will guided by the mind or reason; and that is why we call these bodily cravings our lower self, and our soul with its faculties and desires our higher self. To indulge in the pleasures of the body to excess or merely for their own sake, is beneath the dignity of a human being. He may seek and enjoy them only in so far as they serve the purpose for which God has given them; namely, as a means of attaining our eternal destiny.

From this you can see how important it is for a boy to have a strong character, so that he can keep his lower nature under control and not let his temper or laziness or love of pleasure get control of him. The time when a boy is in the greatest danger of becoming a slave of his lower self is the time of youth or adolescence, that is, the years from around 14 to about 21. One reason why this period of life is so dangerous is that during these years a new appetite or craving makes itself felt that was not felt before. The first stirring of this new appetite marks the beginning of young manhood or what is called the age of puberty, the age at which a boy comes to the full development of his bodily functions or activities. This appetite is called the sexual appetite. In itself it is not bad, but in consequence of original sin it is very often the chief trouble-maker in the fight a young man must make during the years of his growing up. In other words, it is the enemy within the gates that must be kept in chains if a young man wishes to defend the citadel of purity against the assaults of the devil and of the world. It was no doubt to this fight that St. Paul referred when he wrote: "I see another law in my members fighting against the law of my mind" (Rom. 7, 22).

From what you learned in religion class, you know that the virtue of purity requires one to avoid certain looks and touches on oneself and on others: which means that purity requires one to show proper reverence for one's own body as well as for the bodies of others. From the fact that sinful looks at oneself or others and sinful touches or exposure of the body are commonly called immodest looks, touches and exposure, many people think that certain parts of the body must be immodest. Such a conclusion is just as false as the conclusion that wine must be something evil because it can be instrumental in causing the evil of drunkenness. It is not the wine that is evil, but the immoderate use of it; and so, too, no parts of the body are immodest but only the abuse of them.

God created the human body to be a temple of the Holy Ghost; and when our souls are in the state of sanctifying grace, God actually resides in us as in a consecrated temple. And as our soul is in every part of our body, every part of our body belongs to this temple; God dwells in every part of it; every part is sacred and holy and deserving of our reverence. This is true also of those parts which purity requires you to keep hidden, and which for that reason are called the private parts. They are the parts that are different in men and women, and in fact the parts that determine the sex of a human being, making one either a man or a woman, a boy or a girl. Even these parts, I say, are perfectly pure and sacred and deserving of reverence. In Latin they are even called "the parts to be reverenced."

It will be well to recall here what the Bible says on this subject in the story of the creation and fall of our First Parents. It says that God made them male and female, and that they were both naked but were not ashamed. Why were they not ashamed? Because, besides the supernatural gifts of the soul, such as sanctifying grace, God gave them also supernatural gifts of the body, one of which was the immortality of the body, and another, the gift of integrity or original innocence, by which their lower nature was made subject to their higher nature. Without this gift of integrity, Adam and Eve would have had a nature at constant war with itself, the lower nature seeking to satisfy its appetites, and the higher striving to maintain its mastery over the lower.

To prevent this struggle between the higher and the lower part of human nature, God in His infinite goodness gave our First Parents, right from the start, a human nature improved by the addition of the gift of integrity. This gift of integrity put the lower animal part of man, so to speak, definitely in its place by subjecting it completely to the control of the will and the reason. Without that gift Adam and Eve would sometimes have felt inclined to overeat and drink, to be angry or lazy or revengeful and the like; but through that gift their animal nature was made as obedient and submissive to the will as a trained animal that promptly obeys every command of its master.

Like sanctifying grace this gift of integrity was given to Adam conditionally; that is, for only so long as he would keep God's commandment not to eat of the fruit of the tree of knowledge of good and evil. As soon, therefore, as Adam disobeyed by eating the forbidden fruit, both he and Eve lost the gift of integrity; and the immediate result was that their animal passions, which before had been as peaceful as tame animals, now became like wild animals that can be controlled only by being kept in cages or in chains. The Bible clearly indicates these consequences by stating that their eyes were opened and they saw that they were naked. This does not mean that they had been blind before, but merely that the eyes of their mind were opened; and feeling in their bodies the rebellion of the flesh against the spirit, they were deeply humiliated; and sewing together fig leaves, they made themselves aprons to hide their nakedness. Yes, they were so ashamed that when they heard the voice of God walking in the garden, they hid themselves amid the trees.

This Bible account of the fall of our First Parents makes clear why all people who have the normal use of reason have a sense of shame. Shame is the natural result of the rebellion of the flesh against the spirit. And as we have inherited Adam's nature corrupted by sin, we too, are subject to the rebellion of the flesh. And since the sight of the naked body makes one aware of the humiliating fact that our soul no longer has complete control over our animal appetites, there rises a natural desire to hide one's rebellious flesh and a feeling of shame if it is exposed to the view of others. Not merely the inclemency of the weather, therefore, but original sin, or Adam's fall from the state of innocence, was the chief reason why it became necessary for people to wear clothing.

The virtue that regulates man's conduct in regard to the feeling of shame is the virtue of modesty. That is why the conduct of those who give little heed to this instinct of shame is called immodest; and those who disregard it entirely are called shameless. On the other hand, an exaggerated or merely pretended regard for the dictates of modesty is called prudery. Ordinarily in the presence of others, modesty requires that the body be kept covered with the exception of the head and neck, the forearms, and the hands and feet; these parts being the more dignified parts of the body. The upper arms, the legs (especially from the knees up), the back and chest and lower areas are called by Catholic moralists the less seemly parts, which ought not to be exposed except for a good reason.

If the observance of modesty is necessary in general in the presence of others, it is above all necessary in all circumstances and situations in which persons of different sex meet and have dealings with one another. This brings us back to the sexual appetite, of which I said before that it is the chief trouble-maker during the time of your growing up. But as there will be a good deal to say on this subject, I will come back to it in a later instruction, and only add here a reminder to be sure to make regular use of the means of preserving purity that I recommended to you in the last instruction.

INSTRUCTION VII

Listen, son.

If we study the works of God, we see how wisely He has adapted everything to suit its purpose and to attain its end. Thus, to induce us to take the proper amount of food, God gave us an appetite; and to insure the propagation of the human race, He implanted in persons of one sex a natural attraction towards persons of the opposite sex, so that they would be led to seek a mate and enter the state of matrimony.

As the purpose of this mutual attraction between men and women is to lead to marriage, it does not normally make itself felt until boys and girls are of marriageable age. Before they reach the age of maturity, boys do not as a rule care for the company of girls. They prefer to play with boys, and they have a feeling that girls are rather silly and a sort of nuisance. Later on, however, they begin to have a liking and even a preference for girls; and they feel a very decided inclination to find a girl to be their own special friend, or their girl friend, as they call her.

You need not be surprised, then, son, when you notice that your feeling towards girls begins to change; that you feel attracted towards them and enjoy being in their company. That is perfectly normal and to be expected. Yet, though this sex attraction or sex appeal, as it is also called, exists in all normal men and women, it is not so strong that it cannot be resisted or also counterbalanced by other attractions; and hence we find that many men and women prefer to remain single instead of getting married. Some, like bachelors and bachelor girls, remain single because they prefer the greater freedom and lesser responsibility of the single state, or because they want to devote themselves with greater zeal to their chosen profession. Some, too, do not seem to find a partner to suit them. Very many others, however, such as Priests, Sisters, and religious Brothers, remain single in order to be able to give themselves entirely to God and to obtain the higher reward promised by Our Lord to those who embrace the state of virginity out of love for Him. The priesthood and the religious state are the two most sublime states to which people can aspire, and all boys and girls who have the necessary physical, mental and moral qualifications for one of these states should deliberate seriously before choosing any other.

But all young folks, even those who have definitely made up their mind that they will marry some day, should take care to hold their affections in check and guard their hearts from falling in love too soon, that is, before they are experienced enough to assume the burden of rearing and supporting a family and of fulfilling all the other duties of the married state.

A point of special importance for you to know is that this sex appeal produces a stronger reaction in boys than girls. God purposely made men more easily influenced by the attraction of the opposite sex so that they would be moved by it to seek a partner in marriage. That is the reason why a man's passions are more easily aroused than a woman's, and also why the man courts the woman and not the woman the man. On the other hand, God gave women an inborn desire to be sought and loved by men, but at the same time a stronger sense of modesty for their own protection. To men God gave a strong sense of chivalry or knightly honor to induce them to use their greater physical strength and skill to protect women from the attacks and improper advances of wicked men, as well as to enable them to control their own sexual desires.

These facts indicate the natural attitude that all men and women should take towards each other. Just as the quality of modesty and reserve towards men is an ornament in a woman, so is a manly and protective attitude towards women a commendable and desirable trait in a man. Right from the beginning of your young manhood strive to cultivate

this knightly attitude towards all girls and women with
whom you have any dealings. This does not mean that you
should be a lady's man—one that fawns upon women and
flutters about them with dandified attentions. That would
not be manly but ridiculous. It does mean, though, that
you should not act on the belief, which so many act upon
in our day, that girls should be bold, self-assertive and man-
nish in their conduct, speech and attire, and that in consequence men should treat them as on the same footing as
themselves and not show them any special deference and
consideration. The thought that you should habitually
keep in mind in your association with girls and women is
this: that women belong to the sex to which the Blessed
Virgin belongs; and you should respect and esteem all wom-
en on account of the qualities with which God has endowed
their sex and which find in Mary their most perfect ex-
emplification. In other words, see in every woman an image of Mary; and as you revere a picture of Mary even if
it be soiled and torn, so honor Mary by your respectful
conduct towards all women; and in all your relations with
them refrain from everything that a good woman would
resent.

Never for a moment entertain the thought that the more
men and women resemble each other, the better it will be
for society. If God had wanted men and women to be alike
in temperament, disposition and manners, He would not
have made them different. But having decided to create
two mutually complementary sexes, each with its own special functions in society, He gave to each those natural
aptitudes and characteristics that fit them for the proper
performance of their respective work in life. For either men
or women to disregard this fundamental difference and to
repress or stunt the peculiarities of their own sex by striving to acquire qualities peculiar to the opposite sex, is
to go against nature and to make monstrosities of themselves. Don't select your friends, whether boys or girls,
from people of that type.

I must now speak to you about several other phenomena of the period of adolescence which will make their appearance sooner or later. These are of a physical nature and mark the turning point in the development of a boy into a man. One of these is the breaking of the voice or its change from a childish treble to a low masculine pitch. Another is the growth of hair in the armpits and around the sexual organs. More important than either of these two phenomena is the development of a new substance inside the sexual organs. This is a whitish, thickish fluid very similar to certain creamy hand lotions, and it contains substances of great importance for a boy's development into a strong and healthy man.

Since God has constructed our body in such a way that the substances needed in it are usually produced in greater quantity than necessary, a portion of this fluid that is not absorbed into the system is discharged through the sexual member at irregular intervals. This usually occurs in sleep, being occasioned by an exciting dream; and the discharge is accompanied by a pleasurable pulsating movement in the sexual organ. Though this is a natural and normal phenomenon, which happens to all boys and men from the time of adolescence until old age, it is unlawful to give in to and enjoy the pleasant feelings that accompany it. To do so with full knowledge and full consent would be a grievous sin.

As boys do not all develop at the same rate, you cannot know just when you will reach this stage of maturity. It may be when you are 14, and it may not be till you are 16 or even older; and since it occurs in sleep, it might happen without your being aware of it. When it does happen for the first time and you wake up and notice it, turn away at once from the pleasure of it with all your will power as from an enticing temptation; and to strengthen your will, keep repeating some short prayer like "My Jesus, mercy" or "Mary, help me; keep me pure!" If you keep on praying and hold back with your will until the feelings subside, you will not be guilty of sin, no matter how strong or pleasant the feeling may be. Hence you do not have to confess it. If you are in doubt whether you gave some consent or failed to resist completely, just make an act of contrition and you may go to Communion. At your next Confession, if you wish, you can confess it as a doubtful matter.

That it is possible to have those pleasant feelings without taking willful pleasure in them will be clear to you from the following examples. Suppose some candy had been poisoned for some reason or other, and that by mistake you would start to eat it. As soon as you would hear the warning cry, "Don't eat that candy, it's poisoned!" you would spit it out and try to get every bit of it out of your mouth. *But the candy would taste sweet just the same,* even though you were doing all in your power to get rid of it. And so, too, it is with those feelings; they will *feel* pleasant even though you resist them. In fact, that is true of every temptation. It is a bait to entice one; and if there were nothing enticing about it, it would not be a temptation.

When the feelings have died away (they last only a few seconds), you may ask God's forgiveness if you think you may have failed in any way, and then turn around and go to sleep. There is no necessity of your leaving your bed to wash yourself, though you may do so; but always, when you bathe, be sure to wash those parts and that entire region thoroughly yet modestly in the same matter-of-fact way that you wash your face and hands. Your body being a temple of the Holy Ghost, not only due regard for health and cleanliness, but also proper reverence for God's temple, requires that you try to keep it sweet and clean. Whenever the temperature of the room permits, cold water is recommended for washing the parts mentioned: as, indeed, a cold bath in general has a hardening and invigorating effect. Keeping the sexual organs clean is the chief means of preventing itching in those parts. Should you nevertheless be troubled with itching, you should know that there is nothing wrong in touching yourself merely to stop an ordinary itching. Whatever touches are necessary for the sake of health, cleanliness and the like may be made with hesitation. Beyond that, the more strictly you observe the rule "Hands off," the better it will be for you. And, of course, common decency, not to speak of the danger of giving scandal, requires one to avoid all such touches in the presence of others. If there should be a persistent habitual itching at the tip of the sexual member, just let your father know and he can have you see a reliable doctor.

Now don't forget that these matters are not to be talked about with any of your companions. Though it is perfectly proper for you to hear them explained by those who have the duty to instruct you and to warn you against moral dangers, it would be wrong to listen to persons discussing them who have no business doing so, and who have neither the necessary knowledge, prudence, nor tact to speak of them in a becoming manner. So if the talk ever veers in that direction, if you cannot prevent it, unceremoniously walk away.

INSTRUCTION VIII

Listen, son.

In this talk, son, I want to give you some more necessary information about the virtue of purity. As I told you
in a former instruction, there is nothing immodest about
the private parts of the body themselves, because they are
a part of the body that was created to be a temple of the
Holy Ghost. Only the abuse of these parts is immodest and
sinful. But, you might ask, if these parts are not immodest,
why must we cover them? Why all this secrecy about them?
Because the exposure of these parts is likely to excite the
sexual appetite, which may be lawfully gratified only in the
holy state of matrimony. It is these two revealed truths—
the sacredness of the body as the temple of the Holy Ghost,
and the concupiscence or lust of the flesh, resulting from the
sin of Adam, which constitute the twofold and ever exist-
ing reason for the necessity of practicing modesty.

Although there is nothing immodest or immoral about
the sexual organs, it would be false to maintain that there
is *nothing wrong* with sex; and that the idea that sex is
something not quite nice is an insult to the beauty of God's
creation. In comparison with the state of human nature as
God originally created it, there is very decidedly something
wrong with sex; and that something is the concupiscence of
the flesh. Because of the loss of the gift of integrity and the
resulting rebelliousness of man's lower appetites, the sex
appetite no longer exists in man as God created it, but is
aroused by the mere sight of the things it craves. Hence
just as our appetite for food is aroused by the sight of something good to eat and we say it makes our mouth water; so
the sex appetite is aroused by merely seeing or otherwise
perceiving the object of its desire; and the more anyone's
form or person is exposed, the more likely will it arouse the

passions of those who view it, especially if they are of the opposite sex. And though this is true chiefly of real persons, it is true also of wholly or partially nude pictures and statues. This explains why it is so important for both men and women to wear modest bathing suits, above all, when men and women bathe at the same place. And it explains also why it is dangerous to allow one's gaze to linger on indecent pictures and statues.

The fact that very many or even most people show little regard for modesty in our day only proves how pagan they have become in their views and habits. Not every kind of exposure, of course, is necessarily sinful; but Catholic boys should understand that the practice of going about or playing certain games stripped to the waist or in very abbreviated trunks is not in conformity with the requirements of Christian modesty. Surely there is nothing dignified about such scanty attire; but the temple of the Holy Ghost should be attired in a dignified manner. Though custom may somewhat lessen the evil effects, there can be no doubt that the reckless exposure of the body in certain sports and recreations, on the beach, on stage and screen, and in social circles, is the occasion of very many sins against holy purity. And though some people have no evil intentions in following these pagan fashions, they cannot evade all responsibility for being the occasion of sin to others. Others, however, foster and encourage as much exposure of the body as possible, because they want to excite their passions and indulge in unlawful sexual pleasure.

But is there such a thing as lawful sexual pleasure—sexual pleasure that a person may deliberately enjoy without committing sin? Yes, there is; but only for persons who are lawfully united in the married state. I have explained to you that, if married people wish to have a child, the husband must give the wife the marital embrace. It is in connection with this embrace, and only then, and only when this embrace is performed in a way to fulfill God's designs in regard to the married state, that the pleasant sensations in the sexual organs may be indulged in without sin. Hence, for an unmarried person to enjoy those feelings, with full knowledge and full consent of the will, is always a mortal sin; not because there is anything impure or shameful in the pleasure itself, but because it is shameful and impure to consent to it and enjoy it against the will of God when one has absolutely no right to it.

There is nothing at all strange about this distinction because we make similar distinctions in regard to the lawfulness of other pleasures. Thus you may enjoy a chicken dinner on a Thursday, but are forbidden under mortal sin to do so on a Friday. And though you may take a full breakfast when you get up in the morning, you may not do so if you wish to receive Holy Communion that morning. We also make a distinction between the moderate and the immoderate enjoyment of food and drink. To eat and drink moderately for the purpose for which God intended us to eat and drink, is something good. To eat or drink immoderately or to excess is a sin.

Now just as the pleasures of eating and drinking may be lawfully enjoyed only when food and drink are taken in such a way as to achieve the purpose for which God intended them, so also the pleasures of sex may be lawfully enjoyed only when employed in a way to achieve the purposes for which God intended them; namely, the purpose of the married state, the chief one of which is to increase the number of people on earth and the number of saints in Heaven. God's wisdom in attaching pleasure to certain functions, but allowing them only under certain conditions, can be easily seen. How many people would eat and drink enough to preserve their health and strength, if food and drink were not pleasant to the taste? Now as God made food tasty and gave us a great variety of it so that we would not grow tired of always having the same kind, and also gave us an appetite to enable us to enjoy our food, so He also attached a special pleasure to the act by which children are brought into existence, so that men and women would be induced to marry and have children. But if people could lawfully indulge in that pleasure without getting married, or without assuming the burden of having children, comparatively few children would be born, and many of those that would be born to an unmarried girl would be deprived of the support and care of a loving father.

Few people in our day, at least among Christians, will deny that gluttony and drunkenness are shameful vices; and they condemn the practice of those pagans of old who, after stuffing themselves with costly foods and wines, would cause themselves to vomit so that they could eat and drink some more. But impurity is even more shameful than gluttony and drunkenness. The glutton and the drunkard have a perfect right to at least some of the pleasures of eating and drinking, even of drinking alcoholic beverages. They sin only because they go to excess. And married persons have a right to the sexual pleasure that belongs to the proper exercise of the duties and privileges of their state. But an unmarried person has no right whatever to enjoy even the slightest sexual pleasure; and if he indulges in it nevertheless, he usurps an exclusive right of the married state, just as truly as a layman would usurp an exclusive right of the priesthood, if he went into a confessional and heard Confessions, or went to the altar and distributed Holy Communion.

This being true, sexual pleasure must remain a closed book to you as long as you are not married; and the only safe and sensible thing for you to do in the meantime is to put all thought and curiosity about it as far as possible out of your mind. You know what terrible consequences followed from Eve's curiosity about the forbidden fruit. So be careful not to make a similar blunder. *So long as you are not married, sexual pleasure is for you forbidden fruit.* You can be quite sure that, just as the devil came to Eve to seduce her by saying, "No, you shall not die; your eyes shall be opened and you shall be like gods," so he will also come to you to excite your curiosity and arouse the desire for that forbidden fruit. He may even make use of some wicked persons to entice you to sin. But at the first sign of such a temptation, take flight at once and escape his trap by saying: "No, No! That is forbidden fruit! I don't want my eyes opened. Jesus and Mary, help me that I may not do this wicked thing and sin against my God."

A lot of people come to grief, son, because they refuse to heed warnings. Boys especially often think it smart to expose themselves to danger. But it doesn't pay to try to be smart when one's life or soul is at stake. So take my warning and do not think, because you do not see any harm in it, that there can be no harm in touching yourself unnecessarily. You do not act that way in regard to physical dangers. Even though you may not understand what harm there can be in handling dynamite or such an innocent looking thing as nitroglycerine, you heed the warning of others and do not fool with them. Yet, believe me, son, the harm that you might do to your body by fooling with high explosives is nothing compared with the moral damage that might result to your soul from meddling with the private parts of your body. Therefore, whenever you are engaged in the care of your body, as when bathing, dressing or undressing, bear in mind that your body is a temple of the Holy Ghost and treat it with the reverence that a consecrated temple deserves. Remember, too, that your Guardian Angel sees everything you do, and ask him to guard you from ever doing anything contrary to holy purity; for your own efforts will avail you little if you do not implore the grace of God.

It is possible that you may have done something in the past that you now suspect or realize to have been contrary to purity. As long as you did not think it was a mortal sin when you did it, God will not hold you responsible for a mortal sin and you are not obliged to confess it. On the other hand, if you should ever have done anything that you thought was a mortal sin but which from shame you did not confess; or if you should ever do so in the future, by all means make a clean breast of it in your next Confession. You needn't be afraid of the priest or think he won't like you anymore. He takes the place of the Good Shepherd who rejoices when a lost sheep comes back to the fold; and he will admire your humility and sincerity and do all that he can to help you. It is very true that mortal sin is an awful thing and something to be ashamed of, because it causes the death of the soul. But for that very reason one should try to get rid of it as soon as possible by an act of contrition and a good Confession.

PLEASE NOTE:

In the following instructions the parents should nowhere declare or imply that all unescorted company keeping among teenagers is sin either in itself or because it is in all cases bound up with the immediate danger of sexual sin.

What is said here is put as it is to jog the parent awake to the dangers involved, and make it his aim to win the boy's willing cooperation toward avoiding all·dangers rather than running any risks.

PART THREE

(To be read to boys of from 16 to 19 years)

INSTRUCTION IX

My dear son,

It is quite a long time since I read to you the first one of these instructions, and during that time you have been constantly developing both mentally and physically, and I am sure also spiritually. Though you have now crossed the borderline between boyhood and young manhood, it is important for you to realize that you are still a comparatively very young and inexperienced young man. The term young man, you know, takes in not only all boys past fourteen, but also all unmarried men up to thirty; and since there is a vast difference between a boy of sixteen or seventeen and one of twenty-one or twenty-five, it follows naturally that there should also be a difference between the privileges accorded to young men of different ages and circumstances. Not only the time of boyhood but also the whole time of youth is a time of preparation for mature manhood; and as this preparation extends over a number of years, it would be folly to give a boy in his early teens the same freedom that may be granted to a young man of twenty-one or over. The younger boy is not yet prepared for so much freedom. He is not aware of, and above all, he does not realize the dangers of such freedom; and in consequence it is not likely that he will make the right use of it.

That is why Almighty God has imposed on parents the solemn duty of guiding and guarding their children most carefully, especially during the years of adolescence. It would be much easier for parents to let their children do as they please; just as it would be much easier for a pastor or confessor to let his parishioners or penitents do as they please, and not to be continually warning them against dangers and urging them to practice virtue. But just as a pastor is responsible for his people, so are parents responsible for their children; and they will have to render a strict account to God, if through their lack of watchfulness and their easy-going yielding to their children's desires, they are the cause that their children suffer harm.

You see, son, there are still many dangers to the welfare of your body as well as of your soul of which you are unaware. And even if you have perhaps been told of them, you have at least never experienced them; and hence you cannot realize how great the dangers are, but must take the word of your parents and spiritual advisers and avoid those things which they assure you may prove harmful to you.

I have given you an instruction on the chief one of these dangers; viz., that which results from the so-called sex appeal or sex attraction. You will recall that God put this mutual attraction in men and women so that persons of one sex would be attracted to persons of the opposite sex and thus be led to contract marriage at the proper time. God did not give this attraction merely that men and women might enjoy each other's company. No; He gave it to lead up to marriage; and, therefore, if a man or a woman has absolutely no intention or possibility of ever getting married, he or she does wrong to run the risk of arousing a passionate love for one of the other sex and thus becoming exposed to the proximate occasion of sin.

And this risk of becoming exposed to grave danger of sin is incurred not only by those who never intend to or cannot marry (e.g., priests, Sisters, lay persons hindered by a vow or some nullifying impediment), but also by those who do not intend to or cannot marry *within a reasonable period of time*. And the reason is this: Since sex attraction is intended to lead to marriage and after marriage to the marital embrace, if a boy is several years too young to marry and nevertheless begins to associate with individual girls, he runs great risk of falling prematurely in love and of then being led by his passionate attachment to take improper liberties (often called "petting" or "necking") or even to giving a girl the marital embrace. If he does the latter with the girl's consent, they both commit the grave sin of fornication; if he does it by force against her will, he is guilty of a penitentiary offense called rape.

It should not be hard for any boy who has had a Catholic education to understand that such actions between unmarried persons are not at all manifestations of true love, which seeks to promote another's true welfare. They are rather the result of yielding to the physical urge of sex appeal, or, to state it bluntly, to the passion of lust. Yet never imagine that you are too much of a gentleman or too well grounded in virtue to stoop so low as to do anything of the kind. In consequence of original sin, the concupiscence of the flesh or the animal in man is so strong that, if one carelessly exposes oneself to the danger of arousing it, it can easily brush aside all considerations of honor and self-respect and the weak promptings of virtue in order to gratify its eager desires. That is why all spiritual writers warn us that the only way to preserve purity is to avoid the danger, and if we come upon it unawares, to take flight.

So do not deceive yourself by supposing that you are strong enough to resist any temptation. The Holy Ghost tells us: "He that loveth danger shall perish in it" (Ecclu. 3, 27). And in particular beware of supposing that you will be in no danger if you are in the company of a perfectly innocent and virtuous girl. Eve was perfectly innocent and virtuous, too, before she rashly exposed herself to danger. The very innocence of a girl may be the occasion of her and your undoing. Sins of the flesh are far from the thoughts of an innocent and normally good girl; but she desires to be loved; and in her innocence she does not realize that the tender tokens of affection she seeks— terms of endearment, caresses and the like—are likely to stir up quite different emotions in her more animal male companion. In consequence, she may permit caresses which, while not arousing herself, may strongly inflame the boy's passion. And when the vehemence of the boy's desire leads him to overstep the bounds of decency, the girl's loving nature is only too likely to give in and surrender the precious treasure of her purity for the vain satisfaction of being loved.

But even if in some exceptional case there were no danger that a certain boy would sin with a certain girl, he should nevertheless avoid early company-keeping in order to be able to concentrate his attention more successfully on the important duties and tasks of the time of youth. That is one reason, among more fundamental ones, why the Church does not approve of the system of co-education. Young people have enough to do to keep their minds fixed on their books and on acquiring the knowledge and good habits they will need later on, without having their attention divided and weakened by interest in the opposite sex. Just because sex attraction is so strong and, in the time of youth, has the added charm of novelty, if you yield to interest in girls, and to certain girls in particular, while you are still in high school, you can easily become so absorbed in them as to be seriously handicapped in the performance of your duties. And then if you find a girl, as you most probably will, who is specially interested in you, your still weak little head will be so turned that you won't want to listen any more to your parents and teachers, foolishly thinking that, because a girl is interested in you, you are sitting on top of the world and don't need to take advice from anybody.

This may sound absurd and ridiculous to you now, because your judgement is still unbiased by interest in girls. So in order to keep your head clear, let your interest still be directed chiefly towards school, home and church affairs, your sports and boy friends; and until you are old enough to think of marrying, let your contacts with girls be only casual and of passing interest.

Even when you will be old enough to seek a partner for marriage, keeping company will be full of dangers. But if you take proper precautions and have constant recourse to prayer and the sacraments, you can confidently count on God's help and protection. That is by no means the case, however, when boys and girls who are far too young to marry, rashly expose themselves to these dangers merely in order to have a good time. And in their case the dangers are the harder to overcome on account of the weak condition of their undeveloped characters.

I know quite well that there are Catholic writers who assume that it is perfectly all right for boys to make a practice of having "dates" and going around alone with a girl even in their early teens. The only thing they object to is having a "steady," that is, going regularly with the same girl. They try to justify their stand by saying that the world has not stood still, and that boys and girls today are wiser than their parents were in their youthful days; that nowadays boys are facing manhood at fifteen, and that, if parents only instruct them betimes on sex matters, teach them to pray, to receive the sacraments often, and to remember their dignity as members of the Mystical Body of Christ, all will be well and there will be nothing to fear.

Certainly the precautions just mentioned are to be employed by all means; but besides being warned and armed against danger, young folks must also avoid unnecessary occasions of danger. The practice of holding hands, kissing, and taking other liberties is so universal among boys and girls who have dates in these pagan times, that there is every reason to fear that Catholic boys will follow the same custom if they have individual dates with girls. I say, therefore, that if you are too young to go steadily with the same girl, you are too young to be going with girls at all; that is as the escort of an individual girl.

Yes, son, the world has not stood still, but human nature has; and the consequences of original sin are still to be reckoned with. It is greatly to be feared that those Catholics who rely so much on knowledge as a means of overcoming temptations are unconsciously influenced by that naturalism which Pope Pius XI condemned in his encyclical *The Christian Education of Youth.*

INSTRUCTION *x*

Listen, son.

When I warned you against the danger of too early association with girls, I realized quite well that the thought would come to you: "Nearly all the highschool boys I know are going with girls. Are they, then, all doing wrong?" They may not all have fallen into the sins to which they are exposing themselves, and charity requires us not to think evil of them; yet it is nevertheless true, even though they may not know it, that they are doing wrong to expose themselves to such dangers; and experience proves only too often that ignorance does not shield them from the sad consequences of exposing themselves to those occasions of sin. Impress this truth indelibly on your mind, son, and think of it whenever you are asked to follow the crowd: *The fact that something is being done by the majority of people does not make it right.* You sometimes hear or read the saying: "A million people cannot be wrong." A million people *can* be wrong. At the time of the deluge, the whole world, except Noe and his family, was wrong; and at the present time, more than a billion people have wrong ideas and habits in regard to religion and morality. So if we would want to regulate our conduct by what the majority of people are doing, there would–soon be few religious or virtuous people left in the world.

Just consider our own country. We used to call this a Christian country; but if this ever was true, it certainly is not true today. About half the people of the United States do not belong to any church at all; many do not even believe that there is a God; and among those who call themselves Christians there are many who do not believe that Jesus Christ is God. So since a great many Americans are practically pagans; since they do not accept the teachings of the Church regarding purity and the sacredness of the marriage contract; and since they know nothing about the priceless treasure of sanctifying grace and the terrible evil of losing it, is it surprising that they do things that are dangerous to the welfare of their souls, and make nothing of sins which a Catholic knows to be mortal?

If you knew nothing of the value of sanctifying grace and did not believe there was a hell, would you hesitate to commit a mortal sin that would give you a lot of pleasure and not expose you to any undesirable consequences? Well, there are millions of your fellow Americans who know nothing of sanctifying grace and do not believe in hell; and do you think their way of life can be a safe guide for you to follow? Yet it is just the conduct of such pagans and downright atheists that has gradually come to constitute the standard of morality of a vast number of our countrymen.

And when Catholics go to see movies and plays, and read papers, books and magazines that reflect this low moral standard, they, too, become contaminated by these false principles of morality. They gradually come to think that what so many people are doing cannot be so bad; and since we are all more prone to evil than to good, they are only too apt to persuade themselves that the Church is too strict, and that certain practices are not as bad as she says they are. And so it happens that, although they learned at school that they must avoid dangerous occasions of sin, many Catholics try to quiet their conscience by saying that certain indecent shows, improper dances, immodest styles and dangerous intimacies between boys and girls may be indulged in because "everybody is doing it."

I know very well that many boys, if told that they are too young to have girl friends, would say: "Heck! Can't a fellow have any fun at all?" These old fogies want to take all the joy out of life." But such a complaint would be both foolish and unjust. Are boys so helpless that they cannot have any fun without girls? Any real boy would be ashamed to admit that. Why, even men have perfectly respectable and enjoyable social gatherings called "stag parties," at which no women are present. And as to the complaint that parents, priests and others, who object to boys and girls keeping company at an early age, want to take all the joy out of life, nothing could be more unjust. The motive and object of such parents and priests is precisely to safeguard the happiness of young folks by protecting them from the sad consequences of their own imprudent desires.

You know that a child often wants to have something— a knife, a pistol or certain food, which no one who truly loves the child would permit it to have, because it might do itself harm. Now the same is true also of boys and girls who are just entering young manhood and young womanhood. Everybody must admit that the parents of a boy still in his teens have had more experience and know more about life's dangers than the boy himself. And since such a boy cannot reasonably question his parents' love for him nor their motives in placing restrictions on his liberty, he ought to observe those restrictions gladly, and thank Heaven that he has parents who do their duty and strive to promote his real welfare and happiness.

In view of all these facts, my deep fatherly concern for your welfare and happiness prompts me to give you the following advice in regard to your relations with girls: Put out of your mind all thought of keeping company until you are twenty-one years old; that is, till you are old enough to think seriously of marrying and of looking for a suitable partner for life. That is the only way that you can succeed in guarding your heart from being entangled in one of those early love affairs that are so premature and so displeasing to sensible people that they are called by the contemptuous name "puppy loves." And this line of conduct, far from being strange or eccentric, is just as sensible as for a boy to show no interest in real estate. He is not in the market for a house or lot, and hence does not bother to acquaint himself with the different styles, merits and costs of houses. And by that same token, since he is not in the market for a wife, it is equally natural for him not to bother with girls but to let them pass by as the idle wind.

This does not mean that a boy must run away or cross the street in order not to meet a girl whom he spies at a distance; but it does mean that he should not be thinking up and seeking ways and means of meeting them and finding excuses for prolonging such meetings. Neither does it mean that a boy must never meet girls socially at home gatherings or parties in company with other boys and girls in the presence of their parents. What I mean is that there should be no pairing off of one boy with one girl; and that in going to and from such gatherings a boy not of age should not have a girl friend as his companion, but should either go alone, or go with some other boy, or with his sister or brother or parents. It is easy to understand that there is infinitely more danger of a boy and girl growing intimate, exchanging endearments, and of falling in love when they are by themselves than when they are in a crowd. Hence you should not have any individual dates with girls; should not take a girl to a movie, dance or party, or for a street car or automobile ride; and you should on principle and for safety sake so guard your heart and your affections that you will not become involved in any love affair before your twenty-first birthday.

Now, to repeat what I have already told you, don't think for a moment that I don't know that many people, old as well as young, will decry these counsels of mine as old-fashioned and impractical. But nothing that they say will make human nature any less old-fashioned than it has always been, nor remove from early company-keeping the dangers I have pointed out. When so many voices and pens are upholding the pagan customs of our day, it is time that at least one clear voice be lifted to defend thoroughly Catholic standards of social conduct and to inspire high-minded young people to dare to pursue an ideal.

As to the practical objection that it is unsafe for a girl to go home alone, I say it is far more unsafe for a girl of immature character to be taken home by an equally immature boy friend. There is ten times more danger of a girl's losing her innocence when escorted home by such a boy than of her being attacked by some hoodlum when she is alone. Such attacks are usually made on girls who of their own accord accept the attentions of a strange man, not on girls who go about their business. If a girl has no girl friend or elderly person to accompany her home, she should arrange for her folks to meet her when she steps from the bus or streetcar.

A word yet in regard to these meetings of groups of boys and girls. First of all, they should not be frequent and, emphatically, they should not be everyday affairs. Your ordinary companions, whether single or several, should be boys; and gatherings of mixed groups, whether formal or informal, should normally not take place even once a week. The practice of meeting with a group of boys and girls nearly every day after school, at a drugstore or some other convenient place, just to talk; or in the evening, to go riding, bowling, skating and the like, cannot but have lamentable consequences. Average adolescent boys and girls just cannot be thrown together constantly like that without becoming prematurely absorbed in the other sex; and lovesickness, jealously, heartache, distaste for studies, and even more calamitous things are the result.

As one wise mother said in counseling her son: "It is easy enough to run around with girls and do as everybody else does. The silliest sissy can do that. But you have to remain pure. Be polite to all girls, as if they were your sisters; but do not be affectionate with any until there is a question of marrying."* So if some of your friends call you old-fashioned or even sneer at you for following this advice, don't let that distrub you. You can rather afford to smile at and pity their ignorance and delusion; for you are much better informed and wiser than they; and your course of conduct will bring you not only greater blessings, but also greater and more lasting peace and happiness in the end.

*Quoted by Raoul Plus, S.J., in "Radiating Christ."

INSTRUCTION XI

My dear son,

In the instruction that I gave you on purity, I called your attention to the reverence you owe your body as a temple of the Holy Ghost. Ignorance or disregard of this sublime truth is undoubtedly one of the reasons why so many people think that they may use their body as they please without regard for it dignity and sacred character. Added to this, as another cause of the deplorable lack of modesty in so many people, is ignorance or the denial of original sin and its consequences for soul and body.

It is true that the soul's white robe of sanctifying grace, which was lost by the sin of Adam, is restored in Baptism; but the body's robe of innocence as well as its armor of immortality, which were likewise lost through original sin, are not restored in this life. In consequence of this loss, just as it is necessary for man to guard his body with clothing against the inclemency of the weather, so it is also necessary for him to cover his body and its members that his gaze may not fall on objects that stir up his passions, and that he may not become a prey to his own unruly animal desires.

These two facts—the dignity of the body as the temple of the Holy Ghost, and the concupiscence or inordinate animal cravings of the body, demand the observance of certain precautions in regard to the body both in our own private conduct as well as in our relations with others. As I have already warned you how to conduct yourself in the care you must take of your body, I shall now explain how you should act in your dealings and associations with others, in particular, with those with whom the danger is greatest and most frequent; namely, with persons of the opposite sex.

Although, as intelligent beings, we can communicate with one another by signs, speech and writing, still, as beings that have a body as well as a soul, we naturally like to show our feelings also by means of bodily contacts; such as pressure of the hand or a pat on the back. Contacts of a more familiar character, however, are reserved for relatives and intimate friends. Thus you don't walk arm in arm with a boy with whom you have only a speaking acquaintance. Neither do you, except when going into a huddle in sports, put your arm around such a boy's waist or neck. These are demonstrations of regard reserved for close friends. A gentleman does not even offer his hand to a lady to whom he is introducted; and he takes her hand only if she extends it first. And if he is a real Christian gentleman, he will not kiss any girl to whom he is not closely related.

So you see, son, how the practice of respectable people draws a line of distinction between the physical tokens of esteem that they bestow upon persons with whom they come into social contact. Some they greet with a nod; to some they offer their hand; others they may take by the arm; but only close relatives and intimate friends receive the salute of their lips. And the reason very plainly is that in all these tokens of love and regard there are greater or lesser degrees of sacredness, which would be entirely eliminated if the more intimate endearments were bestowed indiscriminately upon all.

It stands to reason, then, that a boy or a girl who is ready to kiss anybody and everybody that he or she feels like kissing, can hardly be depended upon to make an ideal husband or wife. They show themselves too flighty, too cheap. If they set so little value on their kisses as to give them to all kinds of persons, they are apt to indulge in still other liberties that will rob them of their self-respect and in the end destroy their virtue. And when young folks have led such a life before their marriage, there is danger that they will not be content with the love of one person after they are married, but will be led to be unfaithful to their marriage vows.

From this you can conclude what is to be thought of those parties where so-called kissing games are played, and where the sacred character of the kiss is cheapened and degraded by being imposed as a penalty in a game of chance. If you ever think of yourself as a future husband, is the girl you picture as your bride one who has bestowed her kisses on numerous other boys? Or is she not rather a girl who has held her lips in reserve for the boy of her dreams—the boy whom she promised to marry? But if you would like a wife who had saved her kisses for you, is it not only right and proper that you should hold your lips in reserve for her?

Believe me, son, the danger in this business of kissing is not to be brushed aside lightly. The very levity with which so many young people treat the matter of kissing and caressing is one of the chief causes that leads them to indulge in downright impure liberties with each other, and even into the terrible sin of arrogating to themselves while still single the sacred privileges of the married state. Yes, some unmarried young people even perform the marital act together; and if the girl becomes an expectant mother in consequence, in many cases, to hide her sin, she adds the sin of murder to that impurity by mercilessly killing the helpless babe in her womb.

These are terrible things, son, sins in fact that cry to Heaven for vengeance; but they are the natural consequences of that utterly pagan custom of our day of allowing mere boys and girls to keep company as if they were of marriageable age; and not only that, but also according them practically as much privacy in their associations with each other as if they were actually married. And from living side by side with people who have these low moral standards, many Catholics who should know better are also led astray and fall into these same awful sins.

It is hard to explain, but it is a fact that sometimes Catholics are worse than non-Catholics in this respect; and that some non-Catholic boys and girls have higher standards than Catholic ones. Just listen to what the conductor of the woman's department in a non-Catholic daily paper says on this subject, commenting on a letter from a girl named Susie: "A boy told Susie that she is the kind of girl that men forget, and Susie is brokenhearted over the remark. She says she is pretty, a snappy dresser, that she kisses the boys any time they ask her, and can't see anything wrong in it in spite of what old fogies say. She can go to a party and drink hootch, smoke cigarettes, and never forget herself. She doesn't mind if the men do 'neck,' because she can tell them where to get off before they go too far. Wonder if Susie herself has not given a pretty fair picture of the kind of girl that men forget.

"Let's look at this girl you've presented here, Susie. How would you sum her up? Isn't cheap the word? Isn't the cheap girl the one men forget—because there isn't anything about her worth remembering? Men do not forget the girl who puts enough value on herself to repulse their too familiar advances. They do not forget the girl who knows you cannot demand respect by words when your conduct belies your words. In her they brush up against something clean and fine that leaves an impression. The girl they don't forget, Susie, is the one who reminds them of the better stuff they're made of. The cheap girl doesn't. That's why they forget her."

So there you have a writer, not in a paper intended only for Catholics, but in a metropolitan' daily, offering advice to readers of every class, with or without religion, and setting down the girl who is free with her kisses as the cheap girl—the kind that men forget. But if a girl free with her kisses is a cheap girl, then the boy who takes advantage of such a girl is equally cheap and a cad. There is no double standard of morality, one for women and one for men, making actions that would be reprehensible in a girl, permissible or lightly to be excused in a boy. No, the same standard holds for both sexes; and precisely because the man should be the knightly protector of woman, it is wholly unworthy of a man, mean and despicable to trifle with the affection and virtue of various girls and then pretend to be worthy of having a pure and unspoiled girl for his wife.

But how can you escape the fine of a kiss, if it is imposed on you in a game at a party? Simply by refusing to pay it. If any game involving kissing is proposed, let it be known that you will not take part in it. If you thus show that you have courage enough to dare to be different, and state that it is a matter of principle with you, the better class of your companions may side with you and persuade the rest to content themselves wih games more suited to self-respecting young ladies and gentlemen. And even should you unsuspectingly run into such a kissing penalty, who can make you carry it out? Are your companions not young ladies and gentlemen? If so, how can they compel you to kiss a girl? But if they are not ladies and gentlemen, then you will know that you are in the wrong crowd; and in order not to embarrass them further, politely ask for your hat, bid them all a kind good-night and—go home. I don't think Emily Post would frown on this procedure; but even if she should, the code of Sinai is more binding than the code of society.

There is yet one more point that I must call to your attention, and then I will bring this instruction to a close. I spoke before of kissing leading to downright impure liberties. A boy would be guilty of such liberties, if he would touch a girl on her breasts, on her limbs or body close to the private parts and, of course, on the private parts themselves, whether above or beneath the clothing. All such deliberate touches are mortal sins; and so, too, are all actions (kisses included) that are indulged in with sexual pleasure, or which constitute in themselves a proximate occasion of indulging in such pleasure; because the enjoyment of that pleasure has been strictly restricted by Almighty God to the holy state of matrimony.

Not every kiss, of course, between a boy and a girl is always and necessarily a sin. There may be light and hasty kisses indulged in by thoughtless young folks that are not sinful. But the step from such kisses to venially sinful kisses is very swift. And when kisses become eager, ardent, oft repeated or long drawn out, they are pactically always mortal sins, because they naturally arouse sexual pleasure, if not in the girl at least in the boy. That a boy in his teens may sometimes feel like kissing certain girls and keeping company with them is quite natural and to be expected; just as he often feels like doing other things that he should not do. We Catholics know very well that it is not only wrong but obligatory to repress certain animal appetites, and that the practice of repressing such lower instincts plays a most important part in the development of a person's character. "So much progress shalt thou make," says the author of the *Following of Christ*, "as thou dost violence to thyself." So bide your time. Be content to be a boy a while longer, and do not covet the privileges of mature age until by years of restraint you have developed a strong will and steady character.

To conclude, then, son, though you have long known that you must avoid dangerous occasions of sin, you probably did not know how much danger lies in actions so commonly looked upon and represented on stage and screen as harmless tokens of endearment. Hereafter, if anyone tries to make you believe that kissing, embracing, fondly holding hands and similar actions between unmarried persons of opposite sex are perfectly innocent and legitimate pasttime, you will know better; and you will no doubt thank God that you were warned of the danger in time. But as knowledge alone will not save you when you are tempted by the enticements of the flesh, continue to strengthen your will by the devout recital of the three Hail Marys for purity as your morning and evening prayers, and also by the frequent reception of the Sacraments.

My dear son,

In the instruction I gave you on keeping company, I explained that the purpose of courtship is to find a suitable partner with whom to enter the holy state of matrimony; and that, in consequence, boys and girls should not begin to keep company until they are of marriageable age. As you are now nearing the end of your teens, I want to speak to you again on this subject in order to strengthen your determination to follow my advice, and at the same time to counsel you further as to what you should avoid to pass unspoiled through this critical period of your life. I am confident that you don't want to make the same mistakes that thousands of other youths are making, but that you want to be different, and not only not follow the crowd, but even win others away from the crowd to the pursuit of Catholic ideals.

For a proper understanding of the matter of company-keeping it is important first of all to bear in mind that the time of courtship is not a state of life, but a period of transition; and that love-making is not to be engaged in for its own sake or for the sake of the pleasure it affords, but as a preparation for the state of matrimony. Hence if a boy has decided to become a priest or religious, he should not begin to keep company at all.

There is no denying the fact that for the average person whose vocation is the married state, the time of courtship holds some of the sweetest joys of life. But these very joys themselves point to marriage as their culmination; for back of the lovers' present enjoyment of each other is always the thought and the hope that their present all too brief hours of companionship will one day be crowned by a lifelong inseparable union in the home of their dreams.

Now if the time of courtship is to be a time of preparation for marriage, it follows necessarily that when a boy enters that stage of his life, he should give serious thought to the obligations of the married state. Many a boy looks upon the day of his coming of age merely as the day of his complete emancipation from the restrictions of boyhood and the day of his entrance upon a period of absolute independence. Such a view is not only wrong but dangerous as well. A boy who is of age may not simply do as he pleases—go and come as he pleases, but still owes his parents not only love and reverence, but also obedience as long as he remains under the parental roof. Prudent parents will, of course, gradually grant him a considerable amount of independence in order to accustom him to decide and act for himself: but they are still responsible for him and should gently but firmly use their parental authority to shield him from forming dangerous habits and companionships.

The reason why you should give serious thought to the obligations of marriage before you become deeply interested in girls is because, if you do not do so before you fall in love, you will not be likely to do so afterwards. The mentality of a boy in love usually admits of no serious reflection on the sterner things of life; and in consequence he sees no need of preparation for the duties of married life. All the more reason, then, for you to do some serious thinking now. What would you think of a young man who would want to be ordained to the priesthood without having seriously considered the obligations of that state, and without having striven to fit himself for the proper performance of his duties as a priest? But the candidate for the married state also faces most serious and difficult obligations—to himself, to his partner in marriage, to his children, to God and the Church, to his country, and to society at large; and it would be folly for anyone to expect to fulfill all these obligations without having prepared himself for them beforehand.

You are familiar with fairy tales which close the story of happily wedded lovers with the words; "And they lived happily ever after." If the meaning is that their wedded life was an unbroken round of pleasures, then those words do not depict the normal course of marriage in real life. In actual life marriage means crosses and sacrifices, anxieties and disappointments, labor and suffering, just the same as the priesthood and the religious state. And only they who are willing and unselfish enough to sacrifice their ease and comfort for the designs of God and the welfare of others, will find true peace and happiness in matrimony.

What the designs of God are in regard to matrimony are very aptly expressed by the two terms "matrimony" and "conjugal state." Matrimony, from the Latin words "matris munium," means "office of mother"; and the office of mother is none other than the office of bearing and rearing children. You see, then, how wrong it would be to enter the married state with the intention of shirking the very purpose and office of matrimony in order to be able to lead a life of ease and pleasure and personal independence as before. To do that would be just as wrong as for a man to enter the priesthood and assume the office of pastor, and then shirk the duties of his office by refusing to preach, to say Mass, to hear Confessions and to visit the sick.

The word "conjugal" comes from the Latin word "conjugium," which means a joining together by a yoke. A yoke, you know, is not a decoration like a bridal wreath, but something binding two together for a common work. The conjugal state, therefore, is the state of a man and a woman who have assumed together the yoke or obligation of laboring together to achieve the purpose of the married state; namely, the rearing of a family.

It is evident, then, that marriage is not a sinecure but a serious vocation. But that is also the beautiful thing about matrimony, just the same as about the priesthood, that its reward, as far as it is realized here below, comes precisely from the unselfish performance of its obligations. What do you think is the greatest earthly happiness that comes to the young man who enters the married state? What is the greatest thrill of his life? Is it that moment, so sung in story, when the girl of his dreams promises to become his wife and he impresses the first sacred kiss on her chaste maiden lips? No, my son. Is it perhaps that long desired moment when, with wedding bells aringing and amid the organ's trembling tones, he accepts her solemn pledge of fidelity "till death do us part"? Again I say, No, my son. Neither is it the pleasure attending the marital embrace, by which marriage is consummated and the marriage bond made indissoluble. For although in that embrace husband and wife become so completely one that, as the Bible says, they become "two in one flesh," still it is not in the act itself but in the result that God intended to produce through it that a Christian husband finds his greatest joy.

Yes, my son, the supreme thrill that comes to the happily wedded couple is that which fills their souls when they hold their first-born in their arms, and see in it not only the joint product of their love, but also the union of their own very substance into a new human being, in which each can trace the beloved features of the other and which will endure forever as a living monument of their love.

Add to this the parents' further happy thought that by the assiduous performance of their parental duties, by their prayers, their instructions, their wise counsels, training and good example, they can mould this child into a beautiful character that will be a joy to men and angels and give glory to God for all eternity, you will understand clearly how true it is that the most worthwhile and lasting joys of wedded life come from the unselfish fulfillment of the sacred office of parenthood. And in the case of those parents who look upon parenthood as a vocation, this is true not only of the first child, but also of each succeeding one; so much so that one sometimes hears a mother say that her husband carries on about the new baby as if they had never had a baby before.

In contemplating marriage, then, you should be contemplating the vocation of parenthood—a privileged and sublime vocation it is true, but a serious and difficult one as well. Only if you view marriage in this light, will you be likely to escape those pitfalls which so often prove disastrous to young people when they keep company. For, viewing marriage as a serious matter, you will also regard courtship, which leads to marriage, as a serious matter; and in weighing the qualifications of the young women you meet, you will judge of their comparative fitness to be your wife, not by their personal charm or their ability to help you have a good time, but by their ability to bear the yoke of wedded life and fulfill the duties of mother toward your children.

Fortified with this serious outlook on courtship, you will not allow it to degenerate into a dangerous or even sinful though pleasurable pastime. And realizing that the physical endearments, kissing and embracing, which so many indulge in recklessly during this period, may easily become sinful in themselves or proximate occasions of mortal sin, you will on principle not permit them to yourself until you are engaged, and even then only sparingly and with great caution. If you are choice, as you should be, in selecting your girl companions, you may presume that they are in the state of grace and, therefore, temples of the Holy Ghost; and this thought should fill you with a sincere and deep reverence for their person. Indeed, if you take this supernatural attitude towards your girl friend, you will be willing, like the knights of old, to defend her honor at the cost of your life; and you will recoil as from a dastardly deed from the very thought of touching her improperly. Without doubt it was with such a feeling of deep reverence that a certain American soldier in France approached his fiancee to kiss her for the first time, which he did with the permission and in the presence of her parents; for, describing the event to his Chaplain later on, he said: "I felt as if I was going to Holy Communion."

And listen to what a non-Catholic writer says about the object of his youthful love: "What noble deeds were we not ripe for in the days when we loved! What noble lives could we not have lived for her sake! Our love was a religion we could have died for. . . . And, oh, how beautiful she was, how wondrous beautiful! It was as some angel entering the room, and all else became plain and earthly. She was too sacred to be touched. It seemed almost presumptuous to gaze at her. You would as soon have thought of kissing her as of singing comic songs in a cathedral." And then he sighs: "Ah, those foolish days, those foolish days when we were unselfish and pure-minded; those foolish days when our simple hearts were full of truth, and faith, and reverence! Ah, those foolish days of noble longings and of noble strivings!"*

The simplest and surest way of eliminating the dangers of company-keeping is to follow the old-time custom of visiting your girl friends in their homes with other members of the family present, and of not taking a girl out except accompanied by some other girl companion. That is also the surest way of getting an opportunity to study your girl friend and get a true picture of her disposition and character. When she is alone with you, she naturally tries to show herself at her best; there she is sweet and gentle and obliging. But note how she acts toward her parents, brothers and sisters in the home. If there her demeanor changes; if there she frowns and frets and "shows her claws" when she is crossed, you will have a better idea of what her conduct is likely to be toward her husband after she is married.

No matter how widely the practice has spread in this pagan age of permitting unmarried young couples, whether engaged or not, to go driving alone together, to roam the woods alone together, or to sit together by themselves for hours in some lonely place, the practice is to be condemned, because it is a serious occasion of sin and one that cannot be justified as necessary. Every boy and girl whose intentions are honorable should welcome the presence of others as a proof of the innocence of their relations and as a safeguard against their own weakness. The old custom of chaperonage was dictated not only by Christian prudence, but also by plain common sense: and the modern practice,

---

*Jerome K. Jerome in *Idle Thoughts of An Idle Fellow*.

so pernicious in its results, of according young couples almost as much privacy and seclusion as if they were married, is condemned even by decent pagans.

It is idle to say that boys and girls must pray and receive the Sacraments frequently and remember their dignity, and then there will be no danger if they are alone together. To say there will be no danger is to fly in the face of all experience and equivalent to saying that you can put live coals and straw together without danger of fire. Certainly they must pray; *but their first duty is to avoid the danger;* and when that is impossible, then they must use both natural and supernatural means to pass through it unharmed. That means that, should you at any time happen to be alone with a young lady, the way to meet the situation is to avoid physical contacts and, above all, to keep your hands off her person. Remember, as I told you in a previous instruction, that the physical tokens of affection, for which girls have a natural weakness, do not ordinarily have the strong sexual reaction on girls that they have on boys; and, therefore, for your own protection, beware of being allured into what may prove a trap for your virtue.

Once you are engaged, if you must give your fiancee a good-night kiss, do it in the house where you say good-night to everybody else. When a boy kisses his mother or sister good-bye, does he go off into some dark corner where nobody can see him? Why, then, should he want to seek privacy and darkness in order to kiss his girl friend good-night?

Many of your friends would only laugh at these cautions I am giving you; but by observing them, son, you will not only spare yourself many a pang of conscience, but also preserve the physical endearments of love in all their freshness for your married life, where you can indulge in them with a clear conscience for their proper purpose of easing the burdens of wedded life, cementing more firmly the married union, and keeping alive some of the romance of love long after the days of courtship are over.

Having devoted the greater part of this instruction to

impressing upon you the serious nature of marriage and courtship, let me in conclusion help you to realize the sacred character of the marriage act. You will no doubt remember that in a previous instruction I stated that the Sacrament of Matrimony, like the Sacrament of Holy Orders, gives rights and privileges as well as powers and obligations not possessed by those who have not received this Sacrament. Now the great privilege of married couples is to co-operate with Almighty God in bringing new intelligent beings into existence, just as it is the privilege of the priest to co-operate with God in bringing Jesus Christ upon our altars. To bring an immortal being into existence is so solemn an act that when God created the first man, He did not simply say, "Let man be made", as He said, "Let light be made", but calling upon the other two Persons of the Blessed Trinity, He said: "Let Us make man to Our image and likeness." Then, having formed a body out of the earth, He breathed into it an immortal soul, and man was made a living and immortal being, an image and likeness of God Himself.

What a distinction it would have been for the great sculptor Michelangelo if God had said to him: "Come, let us make a living statue of Myself. I will direct you how to make it out of your own materials and with your own instruments; and then I will breathe into it an immortal soul, and it will exist forever as the joint product of your skill and my power."

Such a distinction is actually granted by Almighty God to all parents. In His infinite wisdom God placed in the parents' own bodies the instruments and the materials for making an image of Himself, fashioning their bodies in such a way that in the marital embrace the husband's generative organ fits into that of his wife. And in His infinite love, God ordained that, as a climax to that loving embrace, the precious germ of life is transmitted from husband to wife to be united with a similar substance in her womb for the formation of a tiny human body. In the very same instant that those two elements, the father cell and the mother cell, unite in an eternal embrace to form a body, God creates in it an immortal soul, thus making a living image of Himself, an indestructible link between husband and wife, and an everlasting memorial of their mutual love.

And thus you see, my son, what a wonderful and sacred act the marital embrace is, and what an intimate union God establishes through it between Himself and human nature, between husband and wife, and between parents and their beloved child.

*   *   *

This ends these formal instructions, my son; but don't think now that hereafter I do not want to be bothered with your problems or personal affairs. I shall always be happy to advise you and help you as much as I can. And I sincerely hope that you will continue to confide in me; for you may be sur~ that no one is more interested in your true welfare and nappiness than your dear old Dad.

FINIS